THEODORE ROOSEVELT

EDEN FORCE

THEODORE
ROOSEVELT

FRANKLIN WATTS
NEW YORK / LONDON / TORONTO / SYDNEY
A FIRST BOOK / 1987

Cover photograph courtesy of The Granger Collection, New York.
Photographs courtesy of The Collections of the Library of
Congress: pp. 12, 14, 19, 20, 42, 58, 60, 63, 68, 70, 76, 79;
Theodore Roosevelt Collection, Harvard College Library: pp.
26, 38, 66, 69, 80, 83, 86; #326108, Department Library Services,
American Museum of Natural History: p. 47.

Library of Congress Cataloging-in-Publication Data

Eskin, Eden Force.
Theodore Roosevelt.
(A First book)
Bibliography: p.
Includes index.
Summary: A biography of the twenty-sixth President,
who among other achievements transformed himself from
a sickly youth into a hero of the Spanish-American War.
1. Roosevelt, Theodore, 1858-1919—Juvenile
literature. 2. Presidents—United States—Biography—
Juvenile literature. [1. Roosevelt, Theodore, 1858-1919.
2. Presidents] I. Title.
E757.E68 1987   973.91'1'0924 [B] [92]   86-22481
ISBN 0-531-10313-7

The Author would like to thank
Mr. Wallace Dailey of the Harvard
College Library for his assistance
in locating some source material.
In addition, several people at
the Roosevelt Birthplace Museum
have been helpful.

CONTENTS

THEODORE ROOSEVELT

THE EASTERNER
IN THE WEST

—1—

The West was still wild when Theodore Roosevelt first traveled there. In the 1880s, about fifteen years after the Civil War, the Dakota Territory attracted people who enjoyed rough living. Some of them liked the idea that there were very few law officers around. Most of the people were ranchers or cowboys, and they judged people by their actions and their ability to fit in.

The young Easterner was clearly not one of the usual cowboys in the Dakota Territory. He acted strangely according to Western ways—he shaved, brushed his teeth, and did not swear. He even wore glasses! This was considered so strange in the West that people called him "Four Eyes."

His clothing, too, was an Easterner's idea of Western clothing—much too fancy and expensive. The way he spoke was really funny to their ears. After all, what real cowboy ever said, "Hasten forward quickly there"?

A montage of photos of Theodore Roosevelt taken at various times during his career

Yet this "dude" named Theodore Roosevelt learned to live as a Westerner, and he began to command the respect of the real cowboys. He learned to ride all day in the saddle and still have enough energy to sit around and read or talk in the evenings. Many tough cowboys found it difficult to keep up with him. Before long, the dude had become a good cowboy.

Those who knew him soon found out that Theodore played fair with people, and most of them played fair with him. When they didn't, Theodore took action.

Many stories are told about Theodore Roosevelt and how he dealt with troublemakers. Two of these stories come from his days in the West.

One time, after spending a day looking for lost horses, he stopped at a town called Mingusville to find a hotel for the night. Inside the hotel, a bully with a pistol in each hand was keeping everyone terrified in the ground floor room, which was both a bar and dining room. Roosevelt walked in. The bully saw Roosevelt's glasses and said, "Four Eyes is going to treat!"

Roosevelt ignored him, laughed, and sat down. The man with the pistols repeated, "I said Four Eyes is going to treat!"

Roosevelt stood up and walked over as if he were going to follow the bully's orders. He said, "Well, if I've got to, I've got to." Before anybody knew what was happening, Theodore struck the bully hard on the jaw. The pistols went off, fortunately hurting no one, and the man lay unconscious on the floor. Several men dragged him out to a shed, and the next day the bully left town quickly. The story got around, and people gained respect for Roosevelt.

Another true story left Westerners amazed when they learned about how Theodore Roosevelt had dealt with a gang of horse thieves. The thieves had escaped in a boat they stole from Roosevelt's ranch. Even though the horses were found and returned to their owners, Roosevelt still wanted his boat back. He also wanted to see that the men were brought to justice.

He had two men on his ranch build another boat, which took them three days to finish. A blizzard delayed their departure another three days. Then they packed enough food for two weeks and started down the river after the thieves. They traveled several days in freezing weather and almost gave up, but they finally spotted the stolen boat and snuck up on the men.

"Hands up!" Roosevelt shouted, and he and his friends captured the thieves.

Capturing the thieves turned out to be the easy part. Getting them to the sheriff was harder. In the icy weather, Roosevelt and his two friends needed eight days to travel about 100 miles (160 km). During that time they had to feed and guard their prisoners. Finally, Theodore sent his two friends back to the ranch with the boat. A rancher agreed to drive Roosevelt and the prisoners to the sheriff.

The sheriff and everybody else were amazed! They wondered why Roosevelt had bothered to bring in the prisoners. Because there were so few law officers in the West, most people just shot their prisoners, instead of

*TR dressed in a
deerskin hunting suit*

risking their own lives to see that justice was done. But Theodore Roosevelt had studied law, and he believed that people should obey laws. He explained that even this rough territory would soon become states, and the people would be ruled by law. Roosevelt wanted to be one of the first to see criminals tried and punished fairly and to know that law and order ruled the land.

Most of the men and women who knew him in the West would probably have been amazed to learn that this strong, energetic man had been a weak boy. When Roosevelt was a child, his parents were worried that he might not grow up to live a healthy life. Bullies picked on him, and often his younger brother had to defend him. After a while, Roosevelt realized that he had to make his body strong. He began to understand that strength is a kind of protection. Most people do not bully those who seem strong.

When Theodore Roosevelt became President of the United States, he set out to do the same thing for his country that he had done for himself. He worked to make the country stronger so that others would respect it.

It was through Roosevelt's own efforts that he became the tireless, healthy man who gained respect and admiration in his own country and around the world. Through his efforts, his country also gained increasing respect in the world.

THE FIRST YEARS

2

If you looked for a place in the United States that was as different as possible from the West, you might choose New York City. That is where Theodore Roosevelt, Jr., was born on October 27, 1858, to a wealthy family.

The family lived in a fine house at 28 East Twentieth Street. Their home was filled with expensive, well-made furniture, wallpaper, china, and silver. The heavy, beautiful dining room chairs were covered in black haircloth, which the children found scratchy when they had to eat in the dining room. The parlor, with its beautiful crystal chandelier, was used mostly for company. The children were sometimes allowed in the parlor in the evenings or on rare occasions, such as parties. Most of their time was spent in the nursery.

Living in the house were his father, Theodore Roosevelt, Sr.; his mother, Martha Bulloch Roosevelt; and his older sister, Anna Roosevelt. Grandmother Bulloch and

Aunt Anna Bulloch, his mother's mother and sister, lived with them as well. By the time young Theodore was three years old, he had a younger brother, named Elliott, and a younger sister, named Corinne.

The Roosevelt children all had nicknames. Theodore's was Teedie. His older sister Anna was called Bamie. Elliott was called Ellie, and Corinne was called Conie.

Next door on Twentieth Street lived one of his father's brothers, Uncle Robert, with his wife, whom the children called Aunt Lizzie Ellis, and their children. Grandfather Roosevelt lived a few blocks away in a fine house on Union Square.

Roosevelts had lived in New York since they first arrived from Holland in the 1640s. Grandfather Roosevelt still spoke some Dutch. Teedie's father, grandfather, and uncles were all wealthy merchants who sold glass and mirrors that they brought over from Europe.

Teedie thought his father was the most wonderful man in the world. He was strong and handsome and good to others. He had a beard, and his kind eyes seemed to understand the people they saw. He also demanded that his children behave well and do the best they could. The children tried to be good because they wanted Papa to approve. He spanked Teedie only once, and that was for biting his sister Bamie, when he was four years old.

His mother's family came from a place that was very different from New York. They had a plantation with slaves in the town of Roswell, Georgia. Grandmamma Bulloch

The birthplace of Roosevelt

and Aunt Anna were now living in New York because the plantation was not making enough money. When they had moved, they had left one of their slaves, Daddy Luke, in charge.

Teedie's mother often told him about life on the plantation where she had grown up. She was a good storyteller, and she made the people of her childhood come alive. She told of her brothers and sisters and of slaves like Daddy Luke and Bear Bob. She told of adventures of the people she had known and she described the way her family had lived. Even though she made the stories seem very real, the South she spoke of was so different from the world of New York that it often seemed like make-believe to Teedie.

In 1860, Abraham Lincoln was elected president, and soon afterwards, in 1861, the Civil War began. Teedie's father admired President Lincoln, and he believed in the North and the importance of keeping the country united.

Teedie's mother, however, was a Southerner, and her brothers and many old friends were fighting in the South's army or navy. If her husband joined the North's army, he and her brothers could end up fighting each other.

Theodore, Sr., did not become a soldier, but he had an idea to help the soldiers' families. President Lincoln agreed with him, so Papa spent a lot of time during the war traveling about to the soldiers in the Northern army to get them to send part of their pay home to their families. He was worried about the wives and children who might not have enough money for food and clothing while their men were

The future president

away fighting. Today, many soldiers send their money home, but at the time it was a new idea.

When Papa was at home during the war years, he sometimes invited Northern officers to his home. Grandmamma Bulloch usually excused herself with a "headache." She was too much of a Southern lady to sit down with Northern soldiers.

Teedie wanted the North to win. One day he prayed aloud for the Lord "to grind the Southern troops to powder." His mother didn't like that, and he never said it out loud again.

The three Bulloch women worried about their family and friends in the South. Often when Papa was away, Mama, Grandmamma Bulloch, and Aunt Anna would make packages containing blankets and clothing and soap to send to those they cared about in the South. These packages would have to be sent secretly to get past the Northern troops. The children heard the grownups say that the boxes would have to "run the blockade," but they weren't sure what that meant. Nevertheless, the package days were exciting and full of mystery.

Two of Martha Bulloch's brothers were very important to the South's navy. One of them was James Dunwoodie Bulloch, Uncle Jimmie, an Admiral in the Confederate Navy. He had gone to England to have some warships built for the South. He managed to sneak one of them, the *Alabama*, out of England before the United States could stop it. The *Alabama* did a lot of damage to Northern ships. Another brother, Uncle Irvine Bulloch, served on that ship and was rescued by the British when the *Alabama* went down. Even though Teedie sided with the North, he admired his uncles' bravery.

One day, the Roosevelts got word that Daniel Elliott, Grandmamma's son from her first husband, was dying of tuberculosis in the South. Grandmamma wanted to go to him. Papa tried to help her, but Daniel died in 1862, before she could see him. Grandmamma Bulloch did not want to live to see the South lose. She died in 1864, before the North won the War.

At last, Papa was home for good, and in 1865 the Civil War ended. Soon after, President Lincoln was shot and killed. The country was horrified. A train carried his coffin to many places in the country. There was a funeral parade in New York City on April 25, 1865. The parade marched past Grandfather Roosevelt's house, and the children watched from the windows. Long afterward, Ellie and Teedie remembered "seeing Lincoln."

Unfortunately, the four Roosevelt children were not very healthy. Teedie suffered from asthma, a condition that makes it difficult to breathe. Teedie's attacks were very bad. They came mostly at night, and Theodore, Sr., would sometimes gather his son in his strong arms and order the servants to get the horse and carriage ready for an outing in the fresh air. Then father and son would drive, sometimes for hours, until Teedie could breathe more easily. At other times, he would have to sit up with pillows behind his back. Then Mama would tell him stories to keep him from thinking about how he felt. In those days, the medication people now take for asthma had not yet been discovered, and doctors were not always sure what to do to help.

The children's poor health was one reason the family decided that the children would not go to school, but would learn at home instead. Aunt Anna was their first teacher, and sometimes their friends joined them for lessons. Aunt Anna married a man named James Gracie in 1866, and the Gracies moved into their own house. Bamie taught the younger children for a while. Later Papa hired private tutors to come and teach them.

Since they didn't attend school, the young Roosevelts met very few children outside the family. The three youngest—Teedie, Ellie, and Conie—became close friends. They often thought of their older sister Bamie as one of the adults, not one of the children. They also had their cousins for friends and a few children whose families were friendly with theirs. One of Conie's best friends was a girl named Edith Carow. She lived nearby and often visited to play or study with the Roosevelt children.

Much of what Teedie learned came from reading, and all his life, Theodore Roosevelt would read a lot. His favorite books were about adventures and heroes or about nature. He was too weak and sickly to imagine himself having adventures like those in his books, but he was able to learn more about nature.

THE WONDERS
OF NATURE

Teedie and his brother and sisters always looked forward to the summertime. Late in the spring each year, the family would move out to the country and stay until the fall. Their tutors and lessons went with them. The Roosevelts believed that fresh air in the country would help Teedie's asthma. At first, they went to New Jersey, and later to the Hudson Valley in upstate New York. Finally, the family found a summer home in Oyster Bay, New York.

Teedie loved the country. He could run barefoot and play hard. He could catch frogs and gather apples. This sickly child had enormous amounts of energy, and he would run and climb and walk as if he were the healthiest boy alive. Even so, he still suffered from terrible attacks of asthma.

All the Roosevelt children enjoyed nature. Teedie not only enjoyed the birds, animals, insects, and plants, he paid careful attention and studied them. He learned to recognize

the songs of different birds, and he could identify each bird by its song. He observed the colors of the male and female birds and their habits, foods, and favorite nesting places. He drew the birds he discovered, and he made notes about what he learned.

When he was nine years old, Teedie wrote a little book called "Natural History on Insects." He wrote that all the insects in the book "inhabbit North America." He added, "mostly I have gained their habbits from ofservation." Although he misspelled *inhabit, habit,* and *observation,* he did write careful descriptions. He did not, however, stick to the subject of insects in this book. Some of the creatures he described are fish, shellfish, and birds.

In New York City, Teedie also managed to find nature to study. At that time, the city had no skyscrapers. There were still open places where mice and frogs and other creatures lived. People never knew whether a frog would come popping out of Teedie's hat or a mouse would show up in a dresser drawer.

One day, when he was about seven years old, Teedie saw a dead seal in a store. The owner was selling pieces of it for meat. Teedie used a pocket ruler he had, paper, and pencil to measure the seal, and he wrote the measurements down. He went to look at the seal each day. How he wanted to own it! In a few days, only the head was left, and the shopkeeper gave it to Teedie.

As a young boy, Teedie had such bad asthma his family spent summers in the country, hoping the fresh air would help him.

Teedie kept his natural treasures in drawers and cupboards. When he put some mice in the icebox, some of the servants threatened to quit. His mother threw out the mice, and Teedie was heartbroken. "No, oh, the loss to science—" he cried.

In fact, he was teaching himself to be a very capable naturalist, a scientist who studies nature. His father understood this and gave him a bookcase on the third floor of the house for what Teedie called the "Roosevelt Museum of Natural History." He and his cousins collected items for the museum.

The summer of 1869 was coming, and Teedie was looking forward to going back to the country. But his family had a surprise for him.

TO EUROPE
AND BACK

—4—

The Roosevelt household was in a state of excitement. They were going to Europe! Teedie was ten years old and not very happy to be going. They were planning to be away an entire year! Teedie would miss his friends. Ellie and Conie were not too happy about going either. Only Bamie seemed to be looking forward to the trip.

Like the trips to the country, one reason for the travel was Teedie's asthma. The family hoped that a change of air might be helpful. They also planned to have some European doctors examine the boy and make suggestions.

On May 12, 1869, the family left New York City on the *Scotia*, a paddle-wheel steamboat headed for England. The first stop would allow them to see Uncle Jimmie and Uncle Irvine, his Southern uncles, in Liverpool. His mother was really looking forward to seeing her brothers, who had been forced to leave the United States after the Civil War.

On the *Scotia*, only Teedie did not try to make new

friends among the children. Instead, he found an elderly man, Thomas St. John, who was a naturalist, and as the ship sailed the Atlantic Ocean, they spent many hours discussing their common interest.

On May 21, they landed in Liverpool, England. Their uncles were waiting to greet them. Mrs. Roosevelt was overjoyed to see her brothers, whom she had not seen in years. The children met their uncles and cousins for the first time. This part of the trip was fine.

From there, the family traveled to Scotland and climbed around ruins. The children enjoyed the climbing more than the ruins. Teedie had a wonderful time.

Then they went through museums and castles. Teedie and the two younger children did not like that part of the trip very much. They preferred the outdoors.

They traveled to Belgium, the Netherlands, Germany, Switzerland, Austria, Italy, and France. Their favorite place was Switzerland, where they had a chance to climb the Alps. All of them walked as much as they could. Teedie walked twenty miles one day. Only his father could walk longer distances than Teedie.

It was a mystery to the whole family how this child who often had trouble breathing could get along so well in strenuous activities that most very healthy people could not do.

Several famous doctors in Europe examined Teedie and found that there was nothing wrong with his lungs. There was nothing about his body that could explain why he had his problems. But the doctors also explained that most people with asthma do not have anything wrong that can be found in a physical examination.

Finally the trip was over, and the family returned home.

The children thought that they had traveled enough and never wanted to leave home again.

Teedie's health continued to worry his family. They thought about sending him to Denver, where the air might be better for him, but he was still too young to go alone. The asthma attacks continued and the boy, with his skinny legs, looked weak and sickly.

One day, his father took him aside and said, "Theodore, you have the mind, but you have not the body, and without the help of the body, the mind cannot go as far as it should. You must *make* your body." His father added that it would be hard work, but he knew his son could do it.

That seemed to be what the young boy was waiting for. His mother began to take Teedie and Ellie to a nearby gym to work out on weights and punching bags and bars. Teedie worked hard at building himself up, but he had been so weak for so long that it would take a long time. Soon the family built a gym in their own house so that the boys could work out at home.

The workouts helped, but Teedie still was sickly. After an attack of asthma when he was thirteen years old, he traveled alone to Moosehead Lake, Maine. On part of the trip, he found himself in a stagecoach with two boys his own age. They bullied Teedie. When he returned home, he asked his parents to let him take boxing lessons. He worked very hard at boxing, and after a while gained some skill. He surprised everyone—even his boxing coach—by winning a series of boxing matches as a lightweight. Although the small pewter cup he won as a prize was not worth much, he valued it a great deal.

Boxing and wrestling were sports Teedie enjoyed all his life. He entered boxing matches in college, and continued to box and wrestle even when he was governor of New York state and president. When he was governor, he often practiced wrestling with the middleweight wrestling champion of the United States.

While Teedie was strengthening his body, he continued to work at his natural history and to read adventure stories.

STRENGTHENING
BODY AND MIND

5

For some time, Teedie had wanted a gun. He wanted to be able to shoot birds and animals so that he could keep the skins and study them. It may seem strange that someone who loved animals wanted to kill them, but at that time many scientists did that so that they and others could learn more about the creatures.

Finally, Teedie's father bought him a gun and showed him how to use it. Teedie was very excited and went out with his friends to shoot, but he could not hit anything. He was puzzled. Then his friends read aloud something on a billboard. Theodore knew that something was wrong. He couldn't even see the letters.

He ran home and told his father, who realized Teedie needed glasses. It took a few weeks before the glasses were ready. Teedie finally put them on. "I had no idea how beautiful the world was until I got those spectacles," he declared. Until then, nobody in the family had realized that the boy was nearsighted.

Teedie asked his father for lessons in taxidermy. Taxidermy is the art of preparing animal skins to preserve them or stuff them. The boy studied with Mr. Bell, who had been a friend of John James Audubon, the great artist who painted birds. Teedie learned how to mount and preserve skins.

That was just in time. In 1872, the family was taking another long trip, this time to Egypt and the Holy Land. Teedie was looking forward to it; he would have a chance to study Egyptian birds.

He bought a book on Egyptian birds and learned to use their Latin names, as real scientists did. He took labels with him and carefully filled out each one with the Latin name and date and place of the catch.

In Egypt, the family lived on a kind of houseboat called a *dahabeah*. For a while, Teedie and Ellie shared a room, but Ellie kept complaining about the smell of the chemicals Teedie used for preserving animals. Finally, some of the other guests left the boat, and Ellie was delighted to get his own room.

(In 1882, when the boy Teedie had become a man, he gave more than 600 bird skins from his collection to the Smithsonian Institution in Washington, D.C. The man at the museum who received the skins knew that they came from a boy's collection and, therefore, did not expect much. To his great amazement, he found he had a collection that was worthy of a careful adult scientist, and he thanked Roosevelt for the unexpectedly excellent gift.)

On the trip, Teedie exercised by boxing with Elliott and by walking long distances to see the sights. He also grew very quickly in Egypt. By the time the family left, all his clothing was several inches too small and new clothing had to be ordered.

After leaving the Holy Land, Turkey, and Greece, the family reached Dresden, a city in Germany. Teedie, Ellie, and Conie learned that they were going to stay there with a family named Minkwitz to continue their education. At first Conie was supposed to stay elsewhere, but she was unhappy, and so was permitted to join her brothers. Their cousins John and Maud Elliott were also staying in Dresden. On Sunday afternoons, the cousins got together. They formed a club, which they called the "Dresden Literary American Club," and they wrote stories, poems, and plays to read to each other.

Anna Minkwitz, the German family's daughter, was their teacher. She taught them German and arithmetic. The boys had a strict schedule, which was interrupted when Teedie came down with the mumps. He wrote to his mother, "Picture to yourself an antiquated woodchuck with his cheeks filled with nuts." After the mumps, he had a bad attack of asthma. His mother took him away for three weeks to the Swiss Alps. When he returned, he worked hard to catch up on his studies.

His mother spoke to Anna Minkwitz and wondered what was to become of her Teedie.

"You need not worry about him," Anna Minkwitz answered. "He will surely one day be a great professor, or who knows, he may even become President of the United States."

The family returned to New York and moved to a new house built for them at 6 West 57th Street. That was not all that was new. Because he had not gone to school, but had studied at home, Teedie needed special training to prepare for college. His father found a teacher, Mr. Arthur Cutler, who worked with the young man on his weakest subjects— Latin, Greek, and math. Young Theodore did not have to work as hard at history, geography, science, French, and German. These were subjects he had learned better than most students his age.

All the studying paid off. Theodore took his test for college, and in 1876 he was admitted to Harvard University.

A NEW LIFE

-6-

Harvard was a new experience for Theodore (now getting too old for the nickname Teedie). It was the first time he went to school with other boys. It was also the first chance he had to meet people outside of his family and his family's friends.

He found a room in a boardinghouse, and his sister Bamie decorated it for him. This would be his home for the next four years, from the fall of 1876 to the spring of 1880. Theodore worked, studied, and kept his animals. He still found time for taxidermy. Sometimes his landlady complained about the smells of the chemicals. And one day his tortoise escaped and frightened her.

Theodore also made friends and became interested in dating girls. Then he started choosing his clothing very carefully.

He taught Sunday school, read a lot, went hunting, and played cards. He also kept studying. Natural science—the

study of animals and plants—interested him more than any other subject, but he liked to study them outdoors. At college he studied them mainly through a microscope.

In the summer of 1877, at the age of eighteen, he wrote and printed a booklet called *The Summer Birds of the Adirondacks.* His friend Harry Minot was listed as a co-author, but Theodore had done most of the work. By that time, he knew almost as much as most naturalists in the United States.

Theodore was not sure what he would do when he finished college. He supposed that he would go into business as his father, uncles, and grandfather had done. That summer his father spoke about Theodore's future career. His father explained that he could leave his son enough money so that he could be a naturalist and not have to worry about making a living. But the money he would leave Theodore could not buy some of the extras in life. "In other words," the son said, "I would have enough for bread, but not for butter or jam." If Theodore decided to be a naturalist, he would have to adjust his spending so that it would match his income. His father added that if he intended to work at something that did not earn much money, he should make it a serious career and plan to do the best work there was in him.

Theodore now had a choice. He could follow a career that made a very good living, or he could follow his love of science and not worry about how he would live. He thought

Theodore, at nineteen, in his Harvard boxing uniform

he would choose the career of a naturalist. Theodore returned to school in the fall of 1877 certain that he would be happy with "bread" and not worry about the "butter and jam."

When Theodore came home in December 1877, his father was sick, but he seemed to be getting better by the time the son returned to Harvard.

On Saturday afternoon, February 9, 1878, Theodore received a message to return home quickly. His father was sick again. Theodore rushed to get a train, but by the time he arrived on Sunday morning, his father had died. Theodore couldn't believe it and didn't know how he could go on.

"He was everything to me," the young man wrote. "How I wish I could do something to keep up his name!"

He returned to Harvard two weeks later and worked harder than ever at his schoolwork. He switched from natural science to political history. He finished with good grades in most subjects and then returned to his house, Tranquillity, in Oyster Bay to be with his family.

In September, Theodore decided to go to Island Falls, Maine, with two cousins, Emlen Roosevelt and West Roosevelt. His former tutor had told them about a woodsman and hunter named Bill Sewall who had a cabin for hunters. It took them two days to travel from New York to Island Falls, and when they arrived Theodore had a bad case of asthma.

Sewall took one look at Theodore and was afraid that he would not be able to take the rough living. He was amazed and delighted to find that his unhealthy-looking guest could tramp through the woods and keep going better than his two cousins could. Both Sewall and Theodore had a favorite poem called "The Saga of King Olaf" by

Henry Wadsworth Longfellow. It was a long poem about a Norse hero, and the two of them knew much of it by heart. They recited it aloud as they tramped through the Maine woods.

Bill Sewall and his nephew, Wilmot Dow, whom Theodore met later, became his lifelong friends. Theodore returned to Maine several times in the next few years.

Shortly after returning to school, Theodore was invited to the home of his Harvard friend, Richard Saltonstall. There Theodore met Richard's neighbor and cousin, Alice Lee. After a second visit, Theodore knew he was in love and vowed that he would marry her.

At first Alice was friendly, but not too interested in Theodore. He smelled of chemicals and was not very graceful. When he proposed the following June, she said no. After all, she was only seventeen and was not yet ready to marry.

As if he didn't have enough to do, Theodore began trying to write a book about the War of 1812, the war between the United States and Great Britain. He was particularly interested in the ships and the part they played in that war.

In his last year of college, Theodore had to write a thesis. He wrote his paper about giving men and women equal rights. Women at that time could not vote, and he said that if women wanted to vote they should be allowed to. He added that the idea of allowing women to vote was fair, but he was not sure that it could be made to work. Most of the people at school thought that Theodore's idea was crazy.

When he graduated, his grades were so good that he was elected to Phi Beta Kappa, an honor society for only the best students.

The estate at Oyster Bay, New York

Theodore also kept seeing Alice Hathaway Lee. Finally, in his last year of school, she agreed to marry him. They were married October 27, 1880, on his twenty-second birthday. For their honeymoon he took her to Tranquillity, the family home at Oyster Bay.

Then Mr. and Mrs. Theodore Roosevelt made their home at his family's house in New York City. They would live there, Theodore decided, until he built another house for them at Oyster Bay.

BACK
IN NEW YORK

—7—

By the time he married Alice Lee, Theodore had decided not to be a naturalist. He wanted to make enough money to provide "butter and jam" as well as bread for Alice and any family they would have. He decided that the way to do this was to become a lawyer.

Theodore began to study at Columbia Law School. He walked for three quarters of an hour each morning to school. When classes were over, he walked to the library and did research for the book he had begun writing at Harvard, *The Naval War of 1812*. He returned home in the afternoon in time to take Alice for a drive. In the evenings, the newlyweds often went out.

Politics and government were beginning to interest Theodore. He asked his friends and family how to go about joining the Republican political club. Friends and family were shocked.

"Politicians are so *low!*" they told him. "Our kind of people don't do that."

"But they are the governing class," insisted Theodore. "And I intend to be one of the governing class."

Against his friends' advice, he found out where the local Republican club met, and he began to go to their meetings. Once again, he was an outsider, a rich gentleman among working people.

It did not take long for Theodore to realize that many political activities were not to his liking. Political clubs had jobs to give out, and the jobs often went to friends or supporters, many of whom were not qualified to do the work. The boss of the club could make most of the members vote with him by seeing that they and their friends got jobs or other favors. Many jobs that had to be done in the city could not be done properly because of politicians.

Street cleaning brought Theodore into a disagreement with the club's boss. The streets needed to be kept clean, and a group of citizens demanded a law to enforce keeping the streets cleaner. Theodore Roosevelt made a speech urging the politicians to pass a law requiring street cleaning. Even though the law didn't pass, people liked the way Roosevelt argued, and they remembered him.

Summer was coming, and Theodore took Alice to Europe in May. Their trip took them to Ireland, England, France, Italy, Austria, Germany, and Switzerland. They ended their journey in Liverpool, England. Roosevelt introduced his wife to his uncles.

Uncle Irvine asked him about his book. Theodore said he was having trouble understanding some ideas about ships and sailing. His uncles, who knew a lot about ships, offered their assistance. With help from Uncle Irvine and Uncle Jimmie, Theodore learned what he needed to finish his book.

A short while after the Roosevelts returned to New York, the Republicans needed someone to run for the state assembly to represent their part of the city. Some club members did not like the man the boss wanted. They nominated Theodore Roosevelt for the job.

The politicians took Theodore around to meet some of the voters. The first place they stopped was a saloon. The owner asked Roosevelt if he would treat saloons fairly, and Roosevelt said he would treat saloons and everyone else fairly.

Then the owner said that he thought the money for a license for a saloon was too high. Roosevelt answered, "In fact, I think it is too low."

The politicians got Roosevelt out of the saloon quickly, before he lost any votes. He won the election.

Roosevelt finished *The Naval War of 1812* in December 1881, just after the election, and it was published the following spring, in 1882. Almost everybody who read it said it was the best book on the subject.

He walked into the state Capitol in Albany on January 2, 1882. He was dressed in fine clothing.

"Who's the dude?" asked one lawmaker.

"That's Theodore Roosevelt of New York."

Roosevelt realized that he was the youngest and probably the wealthiest man among them. By now he knew that even though others considered him an outsider, he would stick to his ideas and not vote just to make friends. Sooner or later, people would accept him.

21st Assembly District.

40th to 86th STS., · LEXINGTON to 7th AVES.

We cordially recommend the voters of the TWENTY-FIRST ASSEMBLY DISTRICT to cast their ballots for

THEODORE ROOSEVELT

FOR MEMBER OF ASSEMBLY,

and take much pleasure in testifying to our appreciation of his high character and standing in the community. He is conspicuous for his honesty and integrity, and eminently qualified to represent the District in the Assembly.

NEW YORK, November 1st, 1881.

F. A. P. BARNARD,	EDWARD MITCHELL,
WILLIAM T. BLACK,	WILLIAM F. MORGAN,
WILLARD BULLARD,	CHAS. S. ROBINSON,
JOSEPH H. CHOATE,	ELIHU ROOT,
WM. A. DARLING,	JACKSON S. SCHULTZ,
HENRY E. DAVIES,	ELLIOTT F. SHEPARD,
THEODORE W. DWIGHT,	GUSTAVUS TUCKERMAN,
JACOB HESS,	S. H. WALES,
MORRIS K. JESUP,	W. H. WEBB.

*The election notice of 1881 endorsing
Roosevelt as a New York assemblyman*

One thing Roosevelt quickly understood was that many of the lawmakers did not care about voting for the right thing or the best thing for the people who elected them. They voted the way they were told to vote. Roosevelt planned to be independent. He would vote the way his conscience told him.

One day, he startled many people. He had found out that a judge was dishonest. The judge was taking money in exchange for favors. Roosevelt stood up and asked for an investigation to see if the judge should be removed from office. Roosevelt had found a letter the judge had written to a businessman, and he used the letter to back up what he said.

The lawmakers tried to prevent a vote, and many businessmen and even relatives spoke to Roosevelt to try to get him to keep quiet about the judge. The young lawmaker was not about to give up. He stood up again and made a second speech. This time he named the businessmen whom the judge had helped, and he offered proof of what he was saying. When it was time for the lawmakers to vote for an investigation, Roosevelt had many votes on his side, but not quite enough.

The newspapers, however, started telling the story. People all over the state began to know Roosevelt's name and to know that he was fighting for honesty in government. Also, Theodore Roosevelt was an interesting person for reporters to write about. This was to be only the first of many times that getting the newspapers to print his ideas helped him. When the assembly voted again, it voted for an investigation.

At first, Theodore Roosevelt did not believe laws should be passed telling businessmen how to treat their workers. When a law came up to keep cigarmakers from working at home, he planned to vote against it. Then he agreed to go and look at some of the apartments where cigarmakers lived and worked. What he saw shocked him. He had no idea that people could live in such terrible conditions. Many families lived in small crowded apartments. He saw one apartment that had only one room and two families living in it. The parents and children lived and worked in that one room and hardly ever made enough money for proper food. Theodore had never imagined that kind of poverty. He knew that he would have to vote for the law.

In September 1884, Theodore went out West to the Dakota Territory. Since Alice was expecting a baby, he left her at home with his mother and sisters.

Roosevelt bought a ranch and some cattle. He found two men, Sylvane Ferris and William Merrifield, to run the ranch for him while he was away. He hoped to make money by raising cattle.

Then he returned home before going back to Albany and the assembly. In the legislature, he kept suggesting laws to cut out some of the dishonesty in government. Whenever he could, he returned home to visit Alice, whose baby was due in February.

On February 13, 1885, he received a telegram telling him that Alice had had a baby girl. He planned to return home that afternoon after a bill he had worked on was passed. But then a second telegram came and he left.

Elliott met him at the front door. "There is a curse on this house," he announced. "Mother is dying, and Alice is dying too." Theodore rushed upstairs to take Alice in his arms. It was true. Then he went to see his mother.

His mother died of typhoid fever early in the morning on February 14. Alice died of a kidney disease that same afternoon. It was too much for him to bear. Without warning, two of the people he loved the most had died on the same day.

"The light has gone out of my life," Theodore wrote in his diary.

Everyone felt sorry for him and deeply saddened by the tragic events. There was a large funeral. Even the minister had trouble holding back tears as he spoke.

Meanwhile, someone had to take care of the baby, named Alice Lee after her mother. Theodore's sister Bamie agreed to take care of her.

Theodore finished out his term in Albany and then headed west to the Dakota Territory. He did not think he would ever go back into politics.

BACK IN GOVERNMENT

—8—

The ranch kept Roosevelt busy, and he worked hard at all the jobs Western men were expected to do. He rounded up cattle and fought prairie fires. He served for a while as deputy sheriff. Even though his eyeglasses still surprised people and his way of speaking was considered too fancy for the West, people began to admire him. He learned to fit in by watching how others behaved and then following the actions of those he admired.

His first ranch was called Chimney Butte. When he bought a second ranch, he called it Elkhorn and asked Bill Sewall and Wilmot Dow to come from Maine to run it. Their wives joined them after a while.

Some of Roosevelt's ways reminded people he was not one of them. The clothes he wore were *his* idea of cowboy clothes, and they were much more expensive than what others wore. He worked hard at ranch work, but it did not come easily. Once when he and Sewall and Dow were chopping trees, someone asked Dow how many trees they had cut that day. Roosevelt overheard Dow say, "Well, Bill cut down fifty-three and I cut forty-nine, and the boss, he beavered down seventeen."

Roosevelt looked at the trees. It was true. Unlike the clean cuts made by the other men's axes, his own trees looked as if a beaver had gnawed them.

Theodore wrote magazine articles and books about the West. He wanted the rest of the country to know about the land that would soon become states. In his western books, Roosevelt wrote about the importance of conservation. Conservation means taking good care of forests, animals, and other natural resources so that they will be available for later generations. Roosevelt realized that many animals were already disappearing, and he wanted to warn people that they must be saved. For the rest of his life, Roosevelt would work for conservation.

From time to time, he traveled east to arrange for his books to be published, to take care of other business, and to see his family and friends. On one visit in the fall of 1885, he saw Corinne's friend, Edith Carow, again. Before long, they realized they loved each other, and they secretly decided to marry. When Bamie and Corinne found out about the engagement, he was embarrassed. "I utterly disbelieve in and disapprove of second marriages," Theodore wrote. Yet he loved Edith and he was going to marry her.

He returned to the West. In 1886, the Elkhorn ranch was in trouble. It was losing money. Bill Sewall advised Roosevelt to get out of the ranch business. Roosevelt decided Bill was right, so he closed down the ranch, and the Sewalls and Dows returned to Maine.

Edith was living in London with her mother and a sister.

She decided that she and Theodore would be married there in December 1886.

When Roosevelt returned to New York before going to London, the Republican party asked him to run for mayor. He did not want to, but he agreed. He didn't win the election.

Roosevelt and Edith were married in London and traveled to France and then Italy before returning home. The house Theodore had started to build for Alice at Oyster Bay was now finished. Edith, Theodore, and his daughter Alice would make it their home. Roosevelt called it Sagamore Hill.

In 1889, President Benjamin Harrison offered Roosevelt a job in Washington, D.C. The job was on the Civil Service Commission. Civil service includes most government jobs except for military ones and elected positions. Roosevelt had believed for a long time that people should have to prove that they could do a government job before they took it. His new work might give him a chance to do something about his ideas. He hoped that testing people for skills needed for the job would help the government get good workers.

Roosevelt remained at the Civil Service Commission for six years. During that time, he wrote magazine articles to get people to understand why a good civil service system was important. By the end of six years, he wanted to do something else.

His daughter Alice was soon joined by other children. First came Theodore, Jr., who was known as Ted. Then there were Kermit and Ethel.

When a job on the New York City Police Board was

offered to him, Roosevelt moved his family back to New York. Before long, he became aware that some high-ranking police officers were not honest. He began to fire them. Then he realized that some police officers goofed off when they were supposed to be working.

Roosevelt met a newspaper reporter named Jacob Riis, who had written a book called *How the Other Half Lives*. The book told how the poorest people in New York lived. The two men would walk the city streets together at night. Roosevelt would go looking for policemen who were not doing their jobs. The newspapers found out about this and printed stories and cartoons about him. They started to call him "Teddy," a nickname he did not like, but he knew the nickname meant that people liked him and knew he was doing a good job.

Riis also took Roosevelt to see how poor people lived. Until then, Roosevelt had thought that people could work their way into better lives. But he began to realize that the poor needed help to rise out of their poverty.

After two years, Roosevelt was asked to be Assistant Secretary of the Navy. His book, *The Naval War of 1812*, proved that he knew a lot about naval matters, and it seemed like a good job for him. A strong Navy was important to Theodore Roosevelt, and he was glad to accept the position.

Once again the Roosevelt family moved to Washington. By now another son, Archibald, had been born. One more son, to be named Quentin, would be born in Washington.

THE HERO OF THE
WAR WITH SPAIN

9

In Washington, Roosevelt worked for John D. Long, the Secretary of the Navy. Long was a calm man who was not interested in war. Roosevelt, on the other hand, believed that it was important to have a strong navy and be prepared to fight. Besides, Roosevelt really loved the idea of war.

At the time, Spain had some colonies that were not too far from the United States. The people in Cuba had fought for freedom from Spain and lost. Spain then treated them badly. Americans did not like the way Spain acted in Cuba and Puerto Rico. Most Americans wanted the Cubans to govern themselves.

James Monroe, an earlier president, had made an important statement in 1823. It is known as the Monroe Doctrine. The main idea of the Monroe Doctrine is that Europe should stay out of North and South America, and the United States would stay out of Europe, unless America's rights were in danger. Since that time, the Monroe Doctrine has been an important element in the way the United States deals with other countries.

Many people in this country did not want Spain in Cuba, and they hoped that the United States would fight Spain to help Cuba become free. Then in 1898, the U.S. battleship *Maine* blew up in the harbor of Havana, Cuba. To this day, nobody is sure what caused the explosion, but at the time many Americans blamed Spain. "Remember the *Maine!*" became a slogan for Americans who wanted war.

One day, when Assistant Secretary of the Navy Roosevelt was at his job, he decided to send a message to Commodore George Dewey in the Pacific Ocean and order him to prepare the ships in the Pacific to be ready to fight Spanish ships if there was a war with Spain.

War did come. Roosevelt gave up his job as Assistant Secretary of the Navy and asked for permission to gather and train volunteer soldiers to fight against Spain.

He was offered a position as colonel, but he did not think he deserved it. So, with Leonard Wood as his colonel, Roosevelt was appointed lieutenant colonel. Once people heard that Roosevelt was organizing troops, men who knew him or knew of him asked to join. Many of the volunteers were ranchers and cowboys from the West. Some Indians joined, too. Others were old friends from Harvard and young college boys. Doctors and lawyers also signed up. They all went to San Antonio, Texas, to train. From Texas, they went to Florida and then Cuba.

Some newspaper reporters called these troops "Roosevelt's Rough Riders," and the name stuck. A few days after arriving in Cuba, the Rough Riders fought their first battle. Shortly afterwards, Colonel Wood was promoted to brigadier general and put in charge of a brigade. Roosevelt, who was now a full colonel, was in command of his Rough Riders regiment.

The Rough Riders' most famous battle was fought on July 1, 1898, on Kettle Hill. Teddy bravely led his men up the hill and exposed himself to danger as he marched. The regiment fought off the enemy and took the hill. Then they marched to nearby San Juan Hill and joined the other troops in capturing it. About eighty-nine Rough Riders and many other Americans died in battle. Afterwards, Theodore exclaimed, "Oh, but we had a bully fight!" "Bully" was one of his favorite words.

Because his actions made interesting stories, several reporters wrote about Roosevelt and the battle. Some of the reporters had written before about Roosevelt when he was on the police board of New York. They remembered how readers liked stories about Teddy. People back in the United States read about Roosevelt and his bravery. They saw pictures that artists drew of the battle. Teddy Roosevelt became the most famous hero of the Spanish-American War.

Some of the greatest difficulties came after the fighting was over. There was not enough food or medicine for the men. Roosevelt used his own money to supply what he could. Many soldiers were sick or dying of malaria and yellow fever, and there were not enough doctors. Disease killed more men than the war did, and the hot, wet climate was making their illnesses worse. A cooler climate would ease much of the suffering. Teddy felt that the men should be shipped back home as soon as possible, but the War Department was in no hurry to bring them back to the United States.

Many Army officers were afraid to write letters about

*Col. Roosevelt and his Rough Riders
at the top of San Juan Hill*

how bad conditions were and how angry they were that the soldiers were not brought home. Finally, on August 3, 1898, Roosevelt wrote two letters about the conditions in Cuba. One was signed in a round-robin way by all the commanders. The other letter was even stronger, and it was signed with just one name—Theodore Roosevelt. He saw that the letters were printed in American newspapers before the Secretary of War received them. The idea worked. The soldiers started to come home on August 8.

The ship landed in Montauk, not too far from Oyster Bay. Crowds gathered to greet Roosevelt's ship. He was their hero.

He was also a hero to his soldiers. Long after the war, soldiers who fought with the Rough Riders would write to him or visit him. They admired him for his bravery and for sticking up for his men.

The Republican party was now looking for someone to run for governor of New York state. They recognized that Teddy Roosevelt had long been popular for fighting for honest government, for the poor, and for fairness. Now he was a war hero as well. People would certainly vote for him.

The only trouble with that idea was that one man controlled the Republican party in New York. His name was Thomas Platt. Would Roosevelt do as Platt told him or would he follow his own beliefs? Anybody who knew Roosevelt should have known the answer to that.

When asked how he would act if he were governor, Roosevelt replied, "I have always been fond of the West African proverb, 'Speak softly and carry a big stick. You will go far.'" From that time on, "Speak softly and carry a big stick" was used to describe Roosevelt's actions.

Roosevelt won the election for governor, and before long Platt realized that Roosevelt was not going to follow orders. Roosevelt might agree with Platt sometimes, and then Platt would get his way. But if Roosevelt thought what Platt wanted was wrong, he made his own decisions.

As governor, Roosevelt worked for conservation. He wanted to be sure that our natural resources would continue to be around for the future. Roosevelt also wanted to break up trusts, groups of firms that had combined by a legal agreement to control most of the business in an industry. Governor Roosevelt thought trustbusting laws should break up some of the big trusts. Thomas Platt did not like these ideas.

After two years of Governor Roosevelt, Platt and his friends started to look for a way to get him out of the job. Since Roosevelt was still very popular, they had to find a way that would not upset the people.

They thought about it for a while, and then they had a brilliant idea. President McKinley's vice president had died. McKinley was running again for president and he needed a new vice president. Nobody would complain if Roosevelt had to give up the governor's job to become vice president.

The only trouble was that Roosevelt did not want the job!

Governor Theodore Roosevelt

THE PRESIDENT
AND HIS COUNTRY

—10—

"Under no circumstances could I or would I accept the nomination for the vice-presidency." That is what Roosevelt said and meant. He knew that most vice presidents had no real work to do, and he liked to keep busy. Many of his Western friends, however, wanted him for vice president, and they made their feelings known.

At the Republican party convention, Roosevelt made a speech nominating William McKinley for a second term. That speech moved everyone; it was now impossible to prevent his nomination. There was no choice, Roosevelt had to accept.

At that time, it was not the custom for the candidate for president to go around making speeches for himself. Instead, others were expected to speak for him. During the campaign, Roosevelt traveled through the country speaking for McKinley.

Along the way, he met many of his Rough Riders and

*The 1900 Republican presidential
campaign poster*

other people he had known before. When he met John Brady, who was governor of the Alaska Territory, Brady said to him, "I greet you as the son of your father, the first Theodore Roosevelt." Then Governor Brady explained that he had been a poor newsboy in New York City, and Theodore Roosevelt, Sr., had paid for him to go out West and make a new life.

William McKinley was elected president for a second term, and before long Roosevelt knew that he had been correct. There was nothing to do as vice president.

The Roosevelt family went to Vermont for a vacation in 1901. While attending a luncheon on September 6, Roosevelt received a telephone call. President McKinley had been shot.

Roosevelt rushed to visit President McKinley in Buffalo, New York. He remained there three days until the doctors told him that McKinley would recover. He was glad to hear that, and he joined his family, who were now in the Adirondack Mountains in New York.

Roosevelt's cabin was on the slopes of Mount Marcy. On September 13, as Roosevelt was coming down the mountain, he saw a runner coming up the hill with a telegram. Before he read the message, he knew what it would be. President McKinley was dying.

He rushed to reach Buffalo. It was a stormy night and there was a long hill. Two or three changes of horses took him in a wild ride down the hill. A train was waiting for him. At the bottom of the hill, his secretary was waiting. "Mr. President," he began. McKinley had died.

"It is a dreadful thing to come into the presidency this way," said Roosevelt.

When he reached Buffalo, he took the oath, the youngest person, at forty-two, ever to be president, at the home of some friends. Only three reporters were in the room. Roosevelt asked to let in others who were standing outside. Because of that, stories of his inauguration appeared in many newspapers. Before long, reporters began to call him by his initials, TR.

TR asked all the Cabinet members to stay in their jobs so that the government could continue smoothly, and they agreed. Then he went on to Washington, D.C. He would do his best for the country.

One of the first things he did that angered some people was to invite Booker T. Washington, a famous black educator, to dine at the White House. Many people, especially Southerners, complained. Roosevelt had no patience with that kind of prejudice.

For a while, the new president tried to carry out McKinley's ways. As time went on, TR started carrying out some of his own ideas to improve the country.

He kept working to improve the civil service. He had the idea that any test given for a job should be connected in some way to the work that had to be done.

He encouraged conservation of our nation's forests and animals. Under TR, millions of acres of land became national parks, forests, monuments, and bird sanctuaries.

He also continued trying to break up trusts. In 1902, TR decided that the Northern Securities Company was preventing other companies from doing business. J.P. Morgan, who was head of the company, thought that the Supreme Court would not let the government break up the company, but he was wrong. The Supreme Court agreed with TR.

Roosevelt also helped end a strike of coal miners. They

*TR with famous California naturalist
John Muir (left) on camping
trip in Yosemite Valley in 1903*

were paid so little for their work that most of them could not feed their families and still pay for housing. TR threatened the mine owners that the United States government would take over the mines and run them if the strike wasn't settled.

One of the lesser issues that interested him was simplified spelling. When he gave a speech in 1906 printed in the simplified spelling, the newspapers made great fun of it. One paper wrote, "No subject is tu hi fr him to takl, nor tu lo fr him tu notis."

As president, TR took a more active part in running the country than most presidents before him. Not everybody liked his actions, but many people did. The big test came in 1904 when he ran for president. The people sent him back to the White House by a large margin.

Just because he was president didn't mean that TR stopped having fun. His children played in the halls of the White House, and he took time to play with them.

He still boxed. One day, a boxing partner accidentally punched him in the left eye, causing some blood vessels to break. Little by little, TR lost the sight in that eye, until by 1908, it was completely blind.

"I was glad that it was the left eye," he said. "If it were the right eye, I would no longer be able to shoot."

He went on hunting trips, too. While on one trip, someone asked him to shoot a bear. It was an old bear that had been captured. Roosevelt did not think it was fair to shoot a bear that had been tied up. He refused. The story got confused. People said that he had refused to shoot a baby bear. Then a toymaker wrote him a letter asking if he could call his stuffed bears "Teddy's bears." The president agreed.

Roosevelt and family

*Roosevelt often went out West
to relax while he was president.*

One of the president's favorite sports was what he called "point-to-point" marches. He would start at one place and choose a spot to head for. The main rule was that you had to go straight, not going around anything. You had to climb over whatever was in the way and wade or swim across water if it were in the path. TR had played that game with his family at Oyster Bay. Now he played it with important people in his government and people from other countries.

TR also acted as a father to his niece, Eleanor. Because his brother Elliott had died, Theodore Roosevelt served in his place in 1905 when Eleanor Roosevelt married Franklin Delano Roosevelt, a distant cousin.

The big White House wedding, however, was for TR's daughter Alice. In 1906, Alice married Speaker of the House Nicholas Longworth of Ohio. All the newspapers in America and many throughout the world carried stories and pictures of the beautiful White House bride.

Alice Roosevelt Longworth

THE PRESIDENT
AND THE WORLD

—11—

For many years, European countries and the United States had been interested in building a canal across Central America. The canal was planned to connect the Atlantic and Pacific oceans. Roosevelt knew how important that was. During the Spanish-American War, it had taken too much time to get ships from the Pacific Ocean to the Atlantic.

A canal would be a path for ships to go from one ocean to another in less time and more safely. The United States wanted to build and govern that canal. Even though it was especially important to the United States, it would be open to ships from all nations.

An agreement was made with Colombia for the United States to make a first payment to Colombia of $10 million then and $250,000 each year for ninety-nine years to use the area in Colombia's territory of Panama for a canal. In addition, $40 million was to pay off the Panama Canal

Company. The ruler of Colombia agreed, but the lawmakers of Colombia did not. They hoped to get even more money from another country.

While the disagreements were going on, the people in Panama started a revolution and declared independence on November 3, 1903. Roosevelt sent U.S. warships to the area. Some people thought that the president encouraged the revolution. He claimed that he did not. He did not, however, try to prevent it. Right after Panama declared independence, the United States made an agreement to build the Panama Canal.

Even people who did not like the way Panama became independent agreed that the Panama Canal was an excellent idea. It helped ships travel between the East Coast and West Coast of the United States. It helped ships of every country that sailed between the two oceans, and it is still important today.

The biggest problem in building the canal was yellow fever. TR remembered that in Cuba, Dr. Walter Reed had discovered that mosquitoes spread the disease. Reed's work, carried out by William Gorgas, helped conquer yellow fever in Panama and other countries.

In 1906, TR decided to visit the Panama Canal to see how the work was coming along. He became the first United States president to leave the country while still in office. He believed that the American people should also see what their government was doing, so he brought along photographers and news writers. The stories and pictures in newspapers and magazines helped the citizens feel as if they were a part of the work at the canal.

Other problems developed in the Americas. Several European countries had threatened to send their navies to collect money they said was owed to them by countries in South America. Roosevelt said no. He came up with his own addition to the Monroe Doctrine. It is called the Roosevelt Corollary. It says that the United States will interfere if a country in the Americas owes money and another nation threatens to take over that country. The United States will not allow the foreign country to come in, and will see that any debts are repaid. As a result of that policy, the United States sent troops to some countries in Latin America.

In 1904–1905, Russia and Japan were at war. Russia had no chance of winning, but refused to surrender. Japan won all the battles, but wanted to stop losing soldiers and money. The war was a problem for the entire world. President Roosevelt decided to try to end the conflict.

It was risky for Roosevelt to try to make peace. If he failed, he would look bad in the eyes of the world, but, even worse, failure would make the United States look bad. But if he succeeded, the United States would gain stature and its president would look good. TR decided to try.

The major problem he had to solve was how to keep each country from thinking he favored the other. Even small things could cause trouble. If one country's representative was allowed to walk through a door first, or if one country was mentioned first in a toast, the other country would be insulted. The smallest thing could end the peace talks.

Roosevelt invited four representatives, two from each country, to his presidential yacht, the *Mayflower*. Then he began talking to the head representatives from both countries at the same time. Their talk was very interesting, and neither man noticed that TR had slowly walked with them through a doorway into the dining room. They were in the room before anyone could worry about who would go first.

Then TR said there would be only one toast, and he would make it. "I drink to the welfare and prosperity of the sovereigns whose representatives have met one another on this ship." Neither country could complain about that.

Roosevelt explained to the men that it was in each nation's interest to make peace. Japan wanted money and land as the price for a peace treaty. Russia refused to admit that it had lost and would not pay anything. It looked as if peace would not come. The American people were beginning to worry.

A new kind of boat, a submarine named the U.S.S. *Plunger*, was not far from the presidential yacht. Roosevelt went aboard to inspect it. Then he asked to dive under the sea in the submarine. He was the first president to submerge in a submarine. The story made all the newspapers. People worried about whether TR was putting his life in danger. For a while, the country stopped worrying about the Russians and the Japanese.

Roosevelt sent messages to the Japanese and Russian governments. The representatives met again. Finally, peace was declared and both governments signed the Treaty of Portsmouth on September 5, 1905, which ended the Russo-Japanese War.

For his work in ending that war, Theodore Roosevelt received the Nobel Peace Prize in 1906. TR was the first American to win this prize. He refused to keep the money for himself. He said, "I was able to do it only because I was President of the United States." He gave the money to a group to set up industrial peace in the United States.

Before his term as president ended, TR decided to send U.S. Navy ships around the world. They stopped at different countries. It was one way of showing that the United States had a strong navy. It also was a way of demonstrating that our country had become more important in the world.

Roosevelt decided not to run again for president. The former presidents had served only two terms, and TR had served almost that long. He suggested that William Howard Taft, his Secretary of War, would make a good candidate for president. TR expected that Taft would carry on the same kind of presidency that Roosevelt had.

Theodore Roosevelt had had a good time in the job. "I do not believe that any president has had as thoroughly good a time as I have had, or has ever enjoyed himself as much," he declared.

An English statesman, John Morley, once said, "Do you know the two most wonderful things I have seen in your country? Niagara Falls and the president of the United States, both great wonders of nature."

*President Roosevelt speaking
at a rally in 1907*

THE EX-PRESIDENT

—12—

What does a person do after being president of the United States? Theodore Roosevelt was only fifty-one years old in 1909, when his presidency ended. He was certainly not a man to sit around doing nothing.

A friend suggested that he go to Africa on a hunting trip. He could come home with animals to display in the Smithsonian Institution in Washington, D.C. TR liked the idea so much that three weeks after he left the White House, he was on his way to Africa with his son Kermit and other hunters and scientists. The Roosevelts enjoyed the trip a great deal and came home with thousands of animals, birds, and skins for the museum.

The trip took a year. When Theodore Roosevelt returned, he decided that he did not like the way President Taft was running the country. Taft was forgetting about conservation and some other important Roosevelt ideas. Many Republicans agreed with Roosevelt.

*TR, son Kermit, and naturalists in Africa,
after Roosevelt's presidency ended*

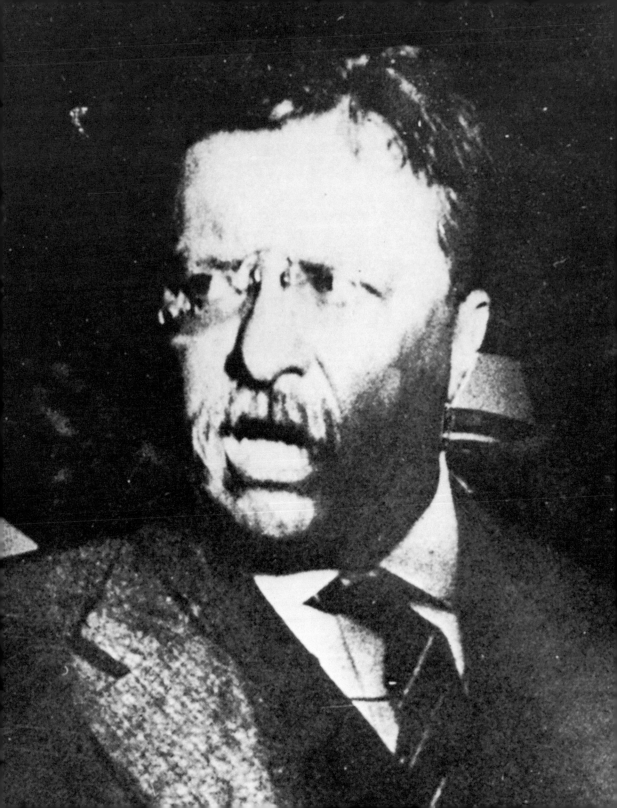

"Maybe I should run for president again," Roosevelt thought.

At the Republican Party convention for the 1912 election, many people wanted to nominate Theodore Roosevelt instead of William Taft. But Taft controlled the list of people who could get into the convention to vote, so he was nominated.

People who wanted Roosevelt were angry. They decided to nominate TR for a different party, the Progressive Party. Many people came to the Progressive Party convention. This was the first time a fairly large political party invited women to vote for their party's candidate at a convention. At this time, women could not yet vote in national elections. Roosevelt promised that if he were elected, he would see that women could vote.

One day a reporter asked TR how he felt. "I feel fit as a bull moose," he replied. After that, people started calling his party the Bull Moose party.

The Democrats chose Woodrow Wilson as their candidate. Now there were three major parties with candidates.

One day, while TR was getting ready to make a speech in Milwaukee, Wisconsin, a man shot him in the chest. Instead of going straight to the hospital, Roosevelt delivered his speech.

This incredible photo shows Roosevelt just a few moments after being shot. He insisted on going ahead with his scheduled speech.

First, he apologized to the audience. "I am going to ask you to be very quiet, and please excuse me from making a long speech. I will do the best I can, but, you see, there is a bullet in my body." He added, "I will deliver this speech or die, one or the other." He spoke for more than an hour.

Then TR went to the hospital. Edith Roosevelt came from Oyster Bay to be with him. The doctors wanted him to rest for several months, but he went on campaigning. Woodrow Wilson won the election, but Theodore Roosevelt received more votes than William Taft.

Once again, Roosevelt had nothing to do. It was time to go on another hunting trip, this time to South America. "It was my last chance to be a boy," he said.

Kermit went with him again. The jungles of Brazil were hot, wet, and filled with insects. The group decided to explore a river nobody knew much about. It was named the River of Doubt. They explored it, and afterwards people renamed it Rio Teodoro, which means "Theodore River."

There was a lot of danger on this trip. Roosevelt injured his leg. Then he became so sick that some of the people on the trip thought he would not live. He did survive, and he returned to America and wrote magazine articles about what he saw.

Meanwhile in Europe, Germany began to show signs of wanting war. Before long, England and France were fighting

These notes for TR's speech and his eyeglass case absorbed some of the shock of the bullet and may have helped save his life.

politics thirty-two years ago to the present time

been that the only safe course t   ue in this country

ours is to treat each man on his w   neither discrimin-

ating in his favor not against him because of his creed or be-

cause of his birthplace.   Thirty-two years ago when I went

into the New York legislature, my close allies in that body

included men like O'Neill, Costello and Kelly, men like Kruse

and Miller, who had themselves been born or whose parents had

been born in Ireland or in Germany and neither they nor I were

capable of considering where the birthplace of any one of us

had been or what creed any one of us professed or what land

his parents came from.   All that any one of us demanded to

know about the others was whether   uare and honest

men, good Americans, devoted to the   ests of our common

country.   During the time I was Police Commissioner of New

against Germany. They wanted the United States to help, but President Wilson worked hard to keep the country out of the war. Roosevelt disagreed. He told President Wilson that the United States should enter the war.

Wilson was re-elected in 1916. Shortly afterward, the United States declared war on Germany after the Germans sank eight U.S. vessels.

Theodore Roosevelt was fifty-eight years old. He had a bad leg and one blind eye. Nevertheless, he wanted to fight in this war. He asked President Wilson to allow him to gather soldiers as he had done in the Spanish-American War and go fight the Germans in Europe. Many men wanted to fight alongside Roosevelt. President Wilson said no, so Roosevelt didn't go.

When the first American soldiers reached Paris and marched down the street, the French people called them the "Teddies." As the soldiers marched, the people of Paris called out, "Long live the Teddies!"

All four of Roosevelt's sons joined the army and went to Europe to fight. He was very proud of them. Pride turned to great sorrow, though, when a telegram arrived saying that on July 14, 1918, Quentin, his youngest son, had been killed. Roosevelt never got over Quentin's death.

On January 6, 1919, Theodore Roosevelt died, beloved by many Americans and people all over the world. His son Archibald sent word to his brothers in France, saying, "The old lion is dead."

EPILOGUE

When Theodore Roosevelt was born in 1858, there were thirty-three states in the United States. By the time he became president in 1901, there were forty-five, and at his death there were forty-eight.

He was born in a time when people rode horses and carriages, steamboats, and trains. By the time he died, automobiles, submarines, and airplanes had been invented. He was the first president to ride in an automobile and fly in an airplane.

Electricity and telephones arrived during his lifetime. So did movies.

Radio and television were not yet a part of his world, but if they had been, he would have used them.

TR grew with the changing times, and some changes came about because of him.

The Panama Canal was one big change. A stronger, more important United States was another. In addition,

Roosevelt was the first modern president of the United States.

He helped save our natural resources and natural wonders. And he saw that the government began to regulate some big companies.

He also contributed to science, geography, and history. Even if he had not been president, Theodore Roosevelt would have been a great American.

One cartoonist said it best: Theodore Roosevelt, American.

FOR
FURTHER READING

Cavanah, Frances. *Adventures in Courage*. Eau Claire, Wisconsin: E.M. Hale and Company, 1961.

Garraty, John A. *Theodore Roosevelt: The Strenuous Life*. New York: American Heritage, 1967.

Judson, Clara Ingram. *Theodore Roosevelt: Fighting Patriot*. Chicago: Follett Publishing Company, 1953.

Quackenbush, Robert. *Don't You Dare Shoot That Bear!* Englewood Cliffs, NJ: Prentice-Hall, Inc., 1984.

INDEX

ABOUT
THE AUTHOR

Eden Force grew up in New York City, where she now lives and works. She earned her B.A. degree in English and American Literature from Brandeis University. The author began writing in her early teens, and her first poem was published when she was thirteen.

Many of the books she now writes deal with American history and government, and they have been used in schools throughout the country. She is co-author of two anthologies of stories and poems for teenagers, and she contributes to dictionaries, as well.

The author has lived for many years down the street from the Theodore Roosevelt Birthplace, a museum and cultural center. When her children were young, she and her husband often took them to concerts and other activities at the Birthplace.